21st Century
Basic Skills
Library

WE CELEBRATE ARBOR DAY IN SPRING

by Jenna Lee Gleisner

Cherry Lake Publishing • Ann Arbor, Michigan

1

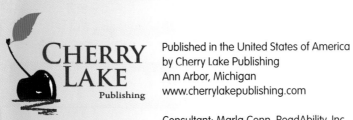

Published in the United States of America
by Cherry Lake Publishing
Ann Arbor, Michigan
www.cherrylakepublishing.com

Consultant: Marla Conn, ReadAbility, Inc.

Photo Credits: Smit/Shutterstock Images, Cover, Title; Vaclav Volrab/
Shutterstock Images, 4; Elias Kordelakos/Shutterstock Images, 6;
EduardSV/Shutterstock Images, 8; Rob Marmion/Shutterstock Images, 10;
Bogdan Wankowicz/Shutterstock Images, 12; Mike Truchon/Shutterstock
Images, 14; Liquidlibrary/Thinkstock, 16; Monkey Business Images/
Shutterstock Images, 18; Matka Wariatka/Shutterstock Images, 20

Library of Congress Cataloging-in-Publication Data
Gleisner, Jenna Lee.
  We celebrate arbor day in spring / by Jenna Lee Gleisner.
      pages cm. -- (Let's look at spring)
  Audience: 5-7.
  Audience: K to grade 3.
  Includes index.
  ISBN 978-1-62431-656-2 (hardcover) -- ISBN 978-1-62431-683-8 (pbk.) --
ISBN 978-1-62431-710-1 (pdf) -- ISBN 978-1-62431-737-8 (hosted ebook)
  1. Arbor Day--Juvenile literature. I. Title.

SD363.G54 2013
634.9--dc23

                                            2013028938

Cherry Lake Publishing would like to acknowledge
the work of The Partnership for 21st Century Skills.
Please visit www.p21.org for more information.

Printed in the United States of America
Corporate Graphics Inc.
January 2014

TABLE OF CONTENTS

5 Spring Season

9 Celebrate

13 We Need Trees

17 Planting

22 Find Out More

22 Glossary

23 Home and School Connection

24 Index

24 About the Author

Spring Season

Spring is here! Days get warmer.

What Do You See?

How many leaves do you see on
the new plant?

Plants and trees grow. It is time for a special holiday.

Celebrate

We **celebrate** Arbor Day in spring. Arbor means "tree."

We celebrate trees on Arbor Day. It is often on the last Friday of April.

We Need Trees

Trees give us shade. They also give off **oxygen**. We need this to breathe.

What Do You See?

What is the robin feeding her baby birds?

Animals need trees, too. Birds and other animals live in them.

Planting

We plant many trees on Arbor Day. Shay plants a tree at home.

Kim's class learns how trees help **soil**. They plant trees at school.

What Do You See?

What does Ian use to plant trees?

Ian's family plants trees. Trees help us all. How do you celebrate Arbor Day?

Find Out More

BOOK

Rissman, Rebecca. *Arbor Day*. Chicago, IL: Heinemann
  Library, 2011.

WEB SITE

Celebrate Arbor Day
www.arborday.org/arborday
Learn more about Arbor Day and different kinds of trees.

Glossary

celebrate (SEL-uh-brate) to enjoy an event or holiday with
  others

oxygen (AHK-si-juhn) a gas with no color that humans and
  animals need to breathe

soil (SOIL) the top layer of Earth where plants grow

Home and School Connection

Use this list of words from the book to help your child become a better reader. Word games and writing activities can help beginning readers reinforce literacy skills.

animals	family	learns	soil
birds	give	live	special
breathe	grow	oxygen	spring
celebrate	help	plants	time
class	holiday	school	trees
days	home	shade	warmer

What Do You See?

What Do You See? is a feature paired with select photos in this book. It encourages young readers to interact with visual images in order to build the ability to integrate content in various media formats.

You can help your child further evaluate photos in this book with additional activities. Look at the images in the book without the What Do You See? feature. Ask your child to point out one detail in each image, such as a color, time of day, animal, or setting.

Index

April, 11

birds, 15

celebrate, 9, 11, 21

holiday, 7

oxygen, 13

planting, 17, 19, 21

school, 19
shade, 13
soil, 19

trees, 7, 9, 11, 13, 15, 17, 19, 21

warmer, 5

About the Author

Jenna Lee Gleisner is an editor and author who lives in Minnesota. She celebrates Arbor Day by planting trees with her family.